W9-BHX-766

Science Alive

Hot and Cold

Terry Jennings

A⁺

Smart Apple Media

Smart Apple Media is published by Black Rabbit Books
P.O. Box 3263, Mankato, Minnesota 56002

Printed in China

Created by Q2A Media
Series Editor: Honor Head
Book Editor: Harriet McGregor
Senior Art Designers: Ashita Murgai, Nishant Mudgal
Designer: Harleen Mehta
Picture Researcher: Poloumi Ghosh
Line Artists: Indernil Ganguly, Rishi Bhardhwaj
Illustrators: Kusum Kala, Sanyogita Lal

Library of Congress Cataloging-in-Publication Data
Jennings, Terry J.
    Hot and cold / Terry Jennings.
       p. cm.—(Smart apple media. Science alive)
    Includes index.
    Summary: "Explains essential facts about temperature, including how it is measured, its effects on weather, and its effects on states of matter. Includes experiments"—Provided by publisher.
    ISBN 978-1-59920-274-7
    1. Heat—Juvenile literature. 2. Thermodynamics—Juvenile literature. 3. Temperature—Juvenile literature. 4. Matter—Constitution—Juvenile literature. I. Title.
QC256.J46 2009
536'.5—dc22
                                                                                        2007050759

All words in **bold** can be found in "Words to Remember" on pages 30–31.

Web site information is correct at time of going to press. However, the publishers cannot accept liability for any information or links found on third-party web sites.

Picture credits
t=top b=bottom c=center l=left r=right m=middle
Cover Images: Main Image: Michael Kelley / Gettyimages   Small Image: Julián Rovagnati / Fotolia: Blwilliamsphoto/ Istockphoto: 4l, Csharrard/ Istockphoto: 5, Olga Lyubkina/ Shutterstock: 6, Eyedias/ Istockphoto: 7l, Dino Ablakovic/ Shutterstock: 7r, Severa777/ Dreamstime: 7b, Index Stock Imagery/ Photolibrary: 10l, Leslie Garland Picture Library/ Alamy: 11, Ian Shaw/ Alamy: 13, kickstand/ Istockphoto: 17, Cephas Picture Library/ Alamy: 18, DuffB/ Istockphoto: 19t, Mauritius Die Bildagentur Gmbh/ Photolibrary: 19br, Index Stock Imagery/ Photolibrary: 22, Wally Bauman/ Alamy: 23, Klemens Waldhuber/ Shutterstock: 25, Martin Jepp/zefa/ Corbis: 28, Blaz Kure/ Shutterstock: 29tl, Vinicius Tupinamba/ Shutterstock: 29tr, Elena Moiseeva/ Shutterstock: 29br, Chen Ping Hung/ Shutterstock: 29bl

9 8 7 6 5 4 3 2 1

Contents

Hot or Cold

Some things are hot. Some things are cold.
A sip of steaming cocoa feels hot in your mouth.
An ice cube feels cold in your hand.

What's hot and what's not?

A campfire is hot enough to cook sausages. A cold shower is lovely on a hot day, but horrible when the weather is freezing. Some foods, such as french fries, are good to eat when they are hot, but taste nasty when they are cold.

◀ *Ice cream is a cold mixture of cream and sugar. Ice cream can sometimes be too cold to eat, and it hurts your teeth.*

Hot and Cold Places

The North Pole and the South Pole are cold all the time. They are covered with ice and snow. Places near the **equator** are hot all year long. Many places between the poles and the equator are cold in winter and hot in summer.

▲ *Polar bears live near the cold North Pole. They have thick fur to keep them warm.*

Temperature

Temperature is a measure of how hot or cold something is. Temperature can tell you if something is hot, warm, cool, or cold.

How a Thermometer Works

We measure temperature with a **thermometer.** A material in a thermometer changes when it is heated or cooled. We read the temperature from the scale.

▲ *The temperature outside can tell us how to dress. On cold days, we wear warm clothes.*

Types of Thermometers

Some thermometers have a red **liquid** in them. Some thermometers are round, like a clock. Digital thermometers have a small window that shows the temperature. Temperature can be measured on either the Farenheit or the Celsius scale. Water **freezes** at 32°Farenheit or 0°Celsius.

▼ *Thermometers often show both Farenheit and Celsius scales.*

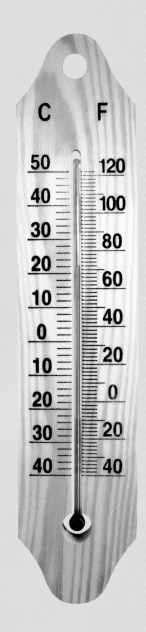

▲ *This thermometer is pointing to 0°Celsius. This is the same as 32°Farenheit.*

Digital thermometer

Try This...
Feeling the Heat

You can find out more about temperature by doing this simple experiment.

You Will Need

• 3 bowls • hot and cold water • ice cubes • a thermometer

1 Ask an adult to fill one bowl with hot water. Use the thermometer to check that the water is about 100°F (38°C). Do not touch the water if it is more than 100°F (38°C).

2 Fill one bowl with cold water and ice cubes. Use the thermometer to check that the temperature is about 32°F (0°C).

3 Fill the third bowl with lukewarm water. The temperature should be about 68°F (20°C).

4 Put one of your hands in the bowl of cold water and the other in the bowl of hot water. Wait about 30 seconds.

5 Then, put both hands in the bowl of lukewarm water. Wait for about 30 seconds.

What happened?

When you put your hands in the lukewarm water, your hands sense the difference in temperature between hot or cold water and lukewarm water. The lukewarm water feels warm to the hand that was in the cold water, but it feels cool to the hand that was in the hot water. Your skin can sense temperature differences, but it cannot tell the exact temperature.

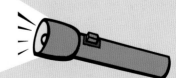

9

What Is Heat?

Like light, sound, and electricity, heat is a type of **energy**. To understand what happens when we heat something, we need to imagine what it is like inside that substance.

Tiny Particles

Everything is made of tiny **particles** that are much too small to see. The tiny particles are moving all the time. Sometimes they move a little, sometimes they move a lot.

◄ *Everything is made of tiny particles that move. When you play with a hula-hoop, you get tired and have to rest. The tiny particles that make up everything never stop moving.*

Adding Heat

Adding heat makes particles move faster. A metal saucepan of water sits on a stove. Heat energy from the stove makes the metal particles move faster and faster. The saucepan gets very hot. The water inside the saucepan also gets hot and it begins to bubble and **steam.**

▲ *The hotter something is, the faster its particles move.*

Heat on the Move

Heat can move from one place to another in different ways. It can even move through empty space.

Convection

The hot air above a radiator rises. Near the ceiling the air cools. It becomes heavier and sinks to the floor. This movement of air around a room is called **convection.**

Hot air

Cool air

▲ *The convection current around a room. You can feel hot air rising if you put your hand above a hot radiator.*

Conduction

A metal spoon becomes hot when it is put in hot soup. The particles in the spoon move faster as they are heated. The particles bump into each other. This movement of heat is called **conduction.**

▼ Heat from the sun travels to you as rays. When heat travels in this way, it is called **radiation.**

Try This...
How Particles Move

You can see how tiny particles move by doing this simple experiment.

You Will Need
• a bowl of water • an eyedropper • food coloring

1 Make sure the water in the bowl is very still. Do not bump or move the bowl.

2 Use the eyedropper to place several drops of food coloring in the water.

3 Watch what happens to the food coloring.

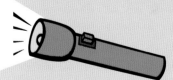

What happened?

The water becomes colored. The coloring is evenly spread throughout the water. This happens even though the water is not stirred. Tiny particles moving around bump into the food coloring. The moving particles mix the coloring in with the water. The coloring finally blends evenly in the water.

Solids, Liquids, and Gases

Materials can be **solids**, liquids, or **gases**. Whether something is a solid, liquid, or gas depends on its temperature.

Cool Solids

A solid has a shape of its own. A brick, a wood table, and an ice cube are solids. The particles in a solid move very little. Heating ice makes the particles move more and the solid ice quickly turns to liquid water.

Runny Liquids

Liquids do not have their own shape. Liquids take the shape of the container they are in. Liquids are runny because their particles move around more than those of a solid.

◀ *Spilled milk runs all over the floor because milk is a liquid.*

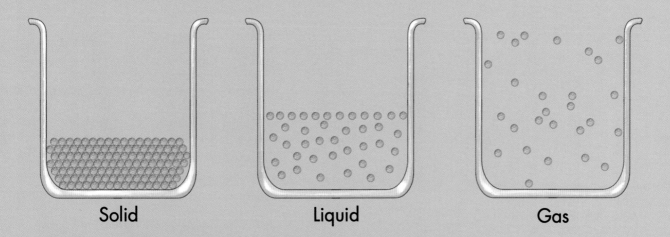

Solid   Liquid   Gas

▲ *Particles are held tightly together in a solid. In a liquid, they are more spread out. In a gas, the particles are free to move very quickly.*

Freeze and Melt

A solid **melts** when you heat it. It changes to a liquid. When you cool a liquid, it turns solid when it reaches its freezing point.

Hot Enough To Melt

Some solids melt easily. If you warm ice cubes, chocolate, butter, or ice cream, they melt. They change into liquids. If you cool these liquids enough, they will change back to solids again.

▲ *When the melted chocolate cools, it will freeze and set hard.*

High Melting Points

Some solids only melt at very high temperatures. Solid iron does not melt until it is heated to 2,876°F (1,580°C). We usually see diamonds as sparkling solids. But even a diamond will melt if it is heated to 6,606°F (3,652°C). That is extremely hot!

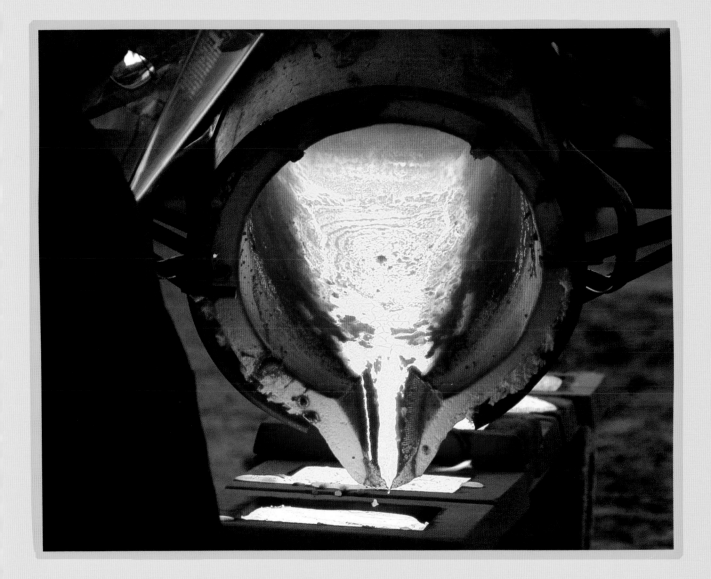

▲ *This liquid iron metal is being poured into molds.*

Try This...
Temperature and Change

You add heat to make things change with this simple project.

You Will Need
• a pan • ice cubes • water • a gas or electric stove

1 Put some ice cubes in the pan.

2 Ask an adult to help you heat the pan on the stove.

3 Keep watching to see what happens to the ice cubes as the burner on the stove adds more heat to the pan.

What happened?

Heat energy makes the water particles move more and the ice melt. This happens when the temperature reaches 32°F (0°C). The stove keeps adding heat energy to the water. As the water heats up, the water particles begin to fly apart. The water turns into a gas called water vapor, or steam. At 212°F (100°C), the water boils.

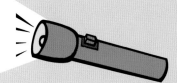

Burn and Boil

Some materials boil when they get hot enough. Different materials have different **boiling points**. Some materials burn when they get hot.

Things That Burn

Many solids, and some liquids and gases, burn when you heat them. Wood, gas, and oil all burn to produce heat energy. They are **fuels.**

◄ *Wood is a material that burns when it gets hot enough. The wood on this campfire is burning and keeping the campers warm.*

Evaporation

Liquids boil when they get hot enough. Water boils at 212°F (100°C). As water is heated, the particles get more and more energy. They move fast enough to turn into **water vapor. Evaporation** is when a liquid turns into a gas.

Condensation

Have you ever seen the bathroom mirror steamed up? Some water from a hot shower turns into water vapor. The vapor cools when it hits the cold mirror and changes back into liquid water. Turning a gas into a liquid is called **condensation.**

▲ *Water vapor from a hot shower has condensed and collected on the mirror.*

Heat and Weather

Warm air is lighter than cold air, and because warm air is light, it rises. When air rises, it helps produce winds and rain.

Winds

The wind blows because the sun warms some parts of Earth more than other parts. The warm land warms the air above it. The warm air rises and cold air rushes to take its place. As the air moves from place to place, it makes a wind.

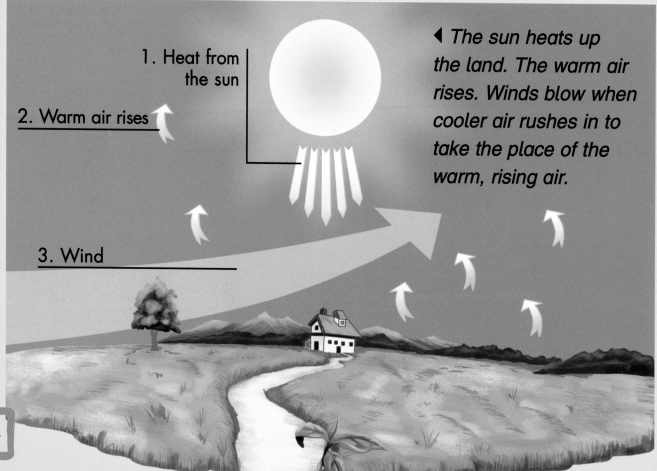

1. Heat from the sun

2. Warm air rises

3. Wind

◀ *The sun heats up the land. The warm air rises. Winds blow when cooler air rushes in to take the place of the warm, rising air.*

Making Rain

The sun shines on the oceans and turns water into water vapor. High in the sky, the water vapor cools and condenses into clouds of tiny droplets. If the clouds cool down further, the droplets join to form bigger drops. The drops fall as rain.

▲ *As warm, moist air rises, it can form huge, towering thunderclouds. When you see dark gray clouds, it is likely to rain soon.*

Try This...

Hot and Cold Air

See what happens to air when it is heated.

You Will Need

• a balloon • a small plastic bottle • a dish • hot water

 Fit the end of the balloon over the opening of the bottle. The balloon must completely cover the opening.

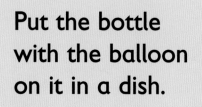 Put the bottle with the balloon on it in a dish.

3 Ask an adult to add hot water to the dish. Watch what happens to the balloon.

What happened?

Heat moves from the water into the plastic and into the air inside the bottle. The air particles move faster and faster. They move farther apart. The air becomes lighter and starts to rise. The only place that the air particles in the bottle can go is into the balloon. The balloon starts to blow up.

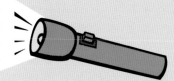

Using Heat and Cold

We use heat to cook our food and to keep us warm. We use cold places to keep our food fresh.

How We Use Cold Places

A refrigerator keeps food cold. You can keep meat, milk, cheese, and other foods in your refrigerator. Refrigerators and freezers take the heat out of food and make it last longer.

A refrigerated truck is like a refrigerator on wheels. It can carry cold or frozen food for thousands of miles.

▶ *Cold temperatures inside the fridge keep food fresh and help stop mold from growing on food.*

Cooking

We heat food to cook it. Cooking changes the way food looks, tastes, and feels. Soft dough turns into crusty bread when it is cooked. Runny eggs turn hard when they are cooked.

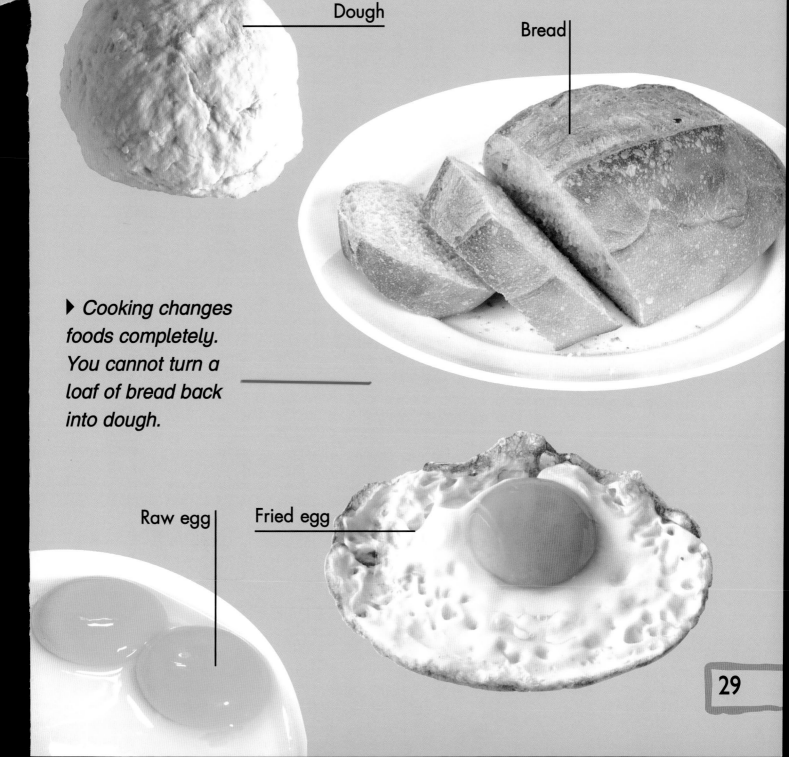

Dough

Bread

▶ *Cooking changes foods completely. You cannot turn a loaf of bread back into dough.*

Raw egg

Fried egg

29

Words to Remember

Boiling point
The temperature at which a liquid turns into a gas.

Condensation
When a gas or vapor changes to a liquid as it is cooled.

Conduction
The movement of heat through a solid material.

Convection
The movement of hot gases or liquids from one place to another.

Energy
The ability to do work.

Equator
An imaginary line around the middle of the Earth.

Evaporation
The change from a liquid to a gas when a liquid is heated.

Freeze
When a liquid changes to a solid.

Fuel
A substance that can be burned to give heat or light.

Gas
A substance with no fixed shape, which spreads in all directions to fill any container it is put in.

Liquid
A material that does not have its own shape, can flow, and takes on the shape of the container it is put in.

Melt

When a solid changes into a liquid. This happens when the solid is heated.

Melting point

The temperature at which a solid changes to a liquid.

Particle

A very tiny piece of matter.

Radiation

The movement of heat rays through space.

Solid

A material that is usually hard, has a shape of its own, and can be cut.

Steam

Water vapor and water droplets that rise from hot water.

Temperature

A measure of how hot or cold something is.

Thermometer

An instrument used to measure temperature.

Water vapor

Water in the form of a gas.

Index

Web Finder

For Kids:

www.harcourtschool.com/activity/states_of_matter/

www.fossweb.com/modulesK-2/SolidsandLiquids/index.html

www.weatherwizkids.com/temperature.htm

For Teachers:

www.k12science.org/curriculum/weatherproj2/en/guidelessons.shtml

www.teach-nology.com/teachers/lesson_plans/science/chemistry/matter/